ETERNAL IMPACT

The Passion of Kingdom-Centered Communities
WORKBOOK

KEN HEMPHILL

STUDY NOTES BY JUDI HAYES

Auxano Press
Tigerville, South Carolina

No part of this book may be reproduced or transmitted in any form or by any means electronic or mechanical, including photocopying and recording, or by any information storage or retrieval system, except as may be expressly permitted in writing by the publisher. Requests for permission should be addressed in writing to Ken Hemphill, Auxano Press; P.O. Box 315; Tigerville, South Carolina 29688.

ISBN 9 781427 627353

Quotations at the beginning of each day's assignment are taken from Eternal Impact: The Passion of Kingdom-Centered Communities by Ken Hemphill (Nashville: B&H Publishing Group, 2007).

Unless otherwise noted, Scripture quotations are taken from the Holman Christian Standard Bible®, copyright © 1999, 2000, 2002, 2003 by Holman Bible Publishers. Used by permission.

Scripture quotations marked NASB are taken from the New American Standard Bible, © the Lockman Foundation, 1960, 1962, 1963, 1968, 1971, 1972, 1973, 1975, 1977, 1995; used by permission.

Scripture quotations marked NKJV are from the New King James Version. Copyright © 1979, 1980, 1982, Thomas Nelson, Inc., Publishers.

To order additional copies of these resources, Ken Hemphill, Auxano Press; P.O. Box 315; Tigerville, South Carolina 29688.

For additional resources for this study, go to www.auxanopress.com or contact Ken Hemphill, Auxano Press; P.O. Box 315; Tigerville, South Carolina 29688.

Printed in the United States of America.

CONTENTS

HOW TO USE THIS BOOK

Warning: This study guide and the accompanying materials contain information that has the potential to change your life. It is our prayer that the Holy Spirit will apply biblical truth with such power that you will live daily with *Eternal Impact.*

Directions: The workbook can be used alone but will have its greatest impact when used with the companion trade book *Eternal Impact: The Passion of Kingdom-Centered Communities,* available from Broadman and Holman Publishing Group.

A DVD, containing 9-11 minutes of a lively question and answer dialogue with Ken Hemphill and Forrest Pollock, is also available. The DVD is designed to stimulate dialogue and thus enhance the learning process.

The material is laid out in a 40 day format, which includes a kick-off event with six weeks of guided Bible study to follow.

It can be used in any small group setting but will have the greatest church-wide impact when used with all youth and adult Bible study participants. We suggest that each participant be given a *workbook* since they will want to record their personal response to God's Word. The trade book should be provided to everyone who will facilitate a small group and made available to anyone in the study. Most churches have discovered that they will need one trade book per family. These are available at a discount rate to your church when ordered by the case. All the teaching tools will be provided at no charge!

Other Free Tools: Teaching tools, administrative guides, and PDF files containing promotional items are free online at any one of the following web sites:

    www.empoweringkingdomgrowth.com
    www.broadmanholman.com/hemphill
    www.auxanopress.com

Kingdom giving and kingdom living are important to author Ken Hemphill. Dr. Hemphill is the National Strategist for Empowering Kingdom Growth of the Southern Baptist Convention. He holds a Ph.D. from Cambridge University and is the former president of Southwestern Baptist Theological Seminary. Other video-driven resources by Ken Hemphill include *EKG: The Heartbeat of God, Making Change: A Transformational Guide to Christian Money Management* and *The Prayer of Jesus*. Other books include *Parenting with Kingdom Purpose*, and the Kingdom Promises devotional series.

INTRODUCTION

Can your church today embrace the dynamics of the New Testament church? Will it embody God's kingdom work in a new way to take the Gospel to the ends of the earth? Can churches today learn from the early church about day-by-day living in relationship with others to worship God, meet others' needs, and spread the Gospel? Can members of your church find again the joy of serving in the kingdom?

The spectacular growth and influence of the early church was not the result of any church growth program or strategy. The Lord Himself drew people to His church. The people had a passion for the lost, for fellowship with God's people, for meeting people's needs, and for living as kingdom believers every day.

He still cares about the church today. Jesus founded the church. He died and was raised to empower it. He sent His Holy Spirit to indwell it, and He is coming again to receive it as His own. He gave the keys of the kingdom to the church. No organization or institution on earth has the mission and significance of the church. God's strategy for the redemption of the nations rests with the church. The key to the transformation of our culture will depend on the church becoming the church. He designed the church to make disciples. And that's still the business of the church today.

In this book we will focus on biblical mandates for becoming all that God intends the church to be. Our focus is spiritual reformation. As you work through the daily readings in this book, you will be challenged to get your heart in tune with the One who brought the church into being. When you open your heart to God, He'll lead you to make a difference for the kingdom.

This book is a companion to *Eternal Impact: The Passion of Kingdom-Centered Communities* by Ken Hemphill (Nashville: B&H Publishing Group, 2007). Your study will be enriched if you read both books together. In that book you'll find thirty chapters that correspond to the thirty days of devotional reading in this book. The five daily readings for each week provide questions to guide you in examining your role in your church and in the kingdom of God.

Also in this book you'll find the outline for a group study. These pages will guide you through the group session. If you are studying on your own, take the time to read the Scriptures and to think about the questions asked.

Think and pray as you read. Apply what you read to your church and to your life. Ask God to open your heart to what He desires most for your church and your role in His church and in His kingdom.

FROM FOUNDATION TO MISSION

Viewer Guide

1. We can live our lives in such a way to have _____ _____.

2. People in the church have _____ and concern.

3. Eighty percent of churches are plateaued or _____.

4. The DNA of the _____ today is found in the early church.

5. Kingdom work is not about progress; it's about _____.

6. Everything begins with the _____.

7. Nothing changes the heart but the _____ of God applied by the _____ of God.

8. The _____ determines everything.

9. God causes the _____.

10. The foundation of the church is _____.

1

11. The church (*ecclesia*) is God's called-out _____.

12. Keys represent access, authority, and _____.

13. Every day can have _____ impact.

Notes

FROM FOUNDATION TO MISSION

The name of this study is *Eternal Impact*. Many things make an impact in our world today. Name some of them. List these. How big is the impact of each? How long does that impact last?

What do you think makes the greatest impact? What makes an eternal impact?

Watch this week's DVD.

1. Talk about a time you were physically lost. How did you feel? What did you do?

Have you used maps from the Internet to help you know each turn to take to reach your destination? Did this increase your confidence in reaching your destination on time?

Have you ever used a GPS (global positioning system) when you drive? How does such a system change your confidence about going to a place you've never been before?

The New Testament book of Acts is God's road map for the church to accomplish God's goal of reaching all people in every nation on earth with the good news of Jesus Christ. With God's guidebook, Acts and other books in the Bible, we can work with confidence in leading and growing our churches.

2. Read Matthew 16:13-19.

Sing or read the words to "Jesus Is the Cornerstone" and "The Church's One Foundation." You can find words for both of these on the Internet.

What do the words of these familiar songs say about Peter's confession and Jesus' response? How would you apply these verses from Matthew's Gospel and the words to these two songs of faith to the church today?

3. Pull your keys out of your pocket or purse. What do they represent? Perhaps they mean ownership of a car or home or business or part ownership as you partner with a lending institution. Or they may mean permission to enter someone else's home or business. In verse 19, what is the significance of the "keys of the kingdom"? Who has them? Who owns the kingdom? Who has permission to use them? What responsibility comes with the permission given to holders of the keys?

4. List types of power.

Recall a time when you "lost power." How did you feel? What did you do?

Read Daniel 7:16; Matthew 7:29; 8:9; 28:18-20; and Ephesians 3:8-11.

What is the source of a Christian's power? What power did Jesus have while on earth? How are Christians today to access and use that power?

5. What divides churches today?

Read Matthew 24:14; 28:18-20; Acts 2:44-47; 4:12; and 2 Peter 3:9.

What mission should unify the church?

If someone were to look at the budget, schedule, and priorities of your church, would they conclude that it exists primarily to complete the discipling of the nations?

What is your church's plan for discipling the nations?

Who does your church partner with to ensure that it has a comprehensive strategy to reach all nations?

Pray that your congregation will be united in reaching your city and the world for Jesus Christ.

THE FOUNDING CONFESSION

"Simon Peter answered, 'You are the Christ,
the Son of the living God." *Matthew 16:16 NASB*

Then as now, this confession—"Jesus is Lord"—is much more than a passing phrase. It has weight It has meaning. It holds eternity in its hands.

Eternal Impact, page 2

Have you ever watched the old Perry Mason legal dramas on TV? The formula for each show ran something like this: A crime is committed, usually a murder. One person is an obvious suspect, though this person is almost never guilty. Perry, often reluctantly, takes the case, even if the person is without funds to pay for his expert legal services. With help from his able assistant, Della, and his detective, Perry searches for the truth. The trial almost always starts without Perry knowing exactly who the murderer is. Sometime during the trial Perry figures it out. While cross-examining a witness, he begins to ask hard-hitting questions that show he knows the person is the murderer. Cornered, the guilty person immediately confesses, both method and motive. The truth finally comes out.

Peter's startling confession in Matthew 16:16 is in some ways similar to the exploits of Perry Mason; for when Peter blurts out the truth, it is as if he has been thinking about it for some time, just waiting for the right moment to shout it out.

Prior to this encounter with his disciples, Jesus had not publicly proclaimed that He was the Messiah, the very Son of God, the long-awaited King of kings and Lord of lords. Earlier in this chapter in Matthew's Gospel, as well as in many other places in the Gospels, the Pharisees and Sadducees are pressing Jesus about who He was and the miracles He did. As He often did, Jesus answered with questions to challenge the speaker about his own faith rather than reveal more about Himself or defend Himself.

Beginning in verse 13, Jesus, having now spent a great deal of time with His disciples, asked them who people said He was. They answered: "Some say 'John the Baptist; and others, Elijah; but still others, Jeremiah, or one of the prophets'" (Matt. 16:14 NASB). They had answered His questions.

Then He asked them directly, "But who do you say that I am?" (v. 15).

Peter, almost always the first disciple to speak or to answer for the group, responded, "You are the Christ, the Son of the living God" (v. 16).

Jesus affirmed the truth of Peter's confession: "Blessed are you, Simon Barjona, because flesh and blood did not reveal this to you, but My Father who is in heaven" (v. 17).

What does the word *confession* mean?

How can that word be used both to admit our guilt and to proclaim the truth?

Peter's confession was that Jesus is the Christ, the very Son of God. What is your confession about who Jesus is?

THE STARTLING ANNOUNCEMENT

*"And I also say to you that you are Peter, and on this rock
I will build My church, and the forces of Hades will not overpower it."*
Matthew 16:18

I believe the church needs this kind of conversation today, because I fear that we are suffering from an identity crisis. We don't understand who we are. Consequently, we don't understand our purpose or our potential. But if we want to recapture the dynamic that enabled the first-century church to turn the world upside down, we must come to a fuller understanding of our biblical identity.

Eternal Impact, page 14

The ad comes on a bright yellow three-inch square attached to the front page of the Sunday newspaper.

Foundation Problems?
Free Estimate
Foundation Repair
House Leveling
Foundation and Structural Solutions Since 1841
167 Years of Service • 167 Years of Excellence

As homes age, they settle, the land shifts, they are bombarded by the elements; and the foundation needs repair. There are telltale signs: Walls or ceilings may have cracks. A pen or pencil seems to roll off every surface. Doors that once closed tightly no longer do. Cakes always come out of the oven with one side thicker than the other.

Sometimes repairs can be costly. Neglect only makes matters worse.

Churches can have foundation problems, too. Church leaders can become so busy with the week-by-week details, organizing Bible study according to the newest guidelines, trying to keep up with the latest worship trends, getting everyone involved in one kind of ministry or another, and scrambling to fill all the teaching and committee positions, that they may forget to make sure the foundation is secure. Every church needs to hear again Peter's confession, "You are the Christ" (Matt. 16:16 NASB) and make sure everything they do is based on that confession and on Jesus' last instructions found in Matthew 28:19-20: "Go therefore and make disciples of all the nations, baptizing them in the name of the Father and the Son and the Holy Spirit, teaching them to observe all that I commanded you; and lo, I am with you always, even to the end of the age." (NASB)

Is your personal foundation of faith secure? Or has it shifted due to distance from Christ or neglect in your relationship with Him? If so, develop a plan for repairing your relationship.

What indications do you see that your church is or is not on a firm foundation of faith in Jesus alone?

Read 1 Corinthians 3:5-15. What does Paul say about the church's one foundation? How did Paul see his role? How do you see yours?

THE STEWARD OF THE KEYS

"I will give you the keys of the kingdom of heaven, and whatever you bind on earth is already bound in heaven, and whatever you loose on earth is already loosed in heaven." *Matthew 16:19*

Make no mistake: the authority of the keys belongs to the King alone. But He has chosen to place this sacred trust in the care of His disciples, who at the time of Matthew 16 were being constituted as His church, His called-out community. And just as surely, these keys remain the privilege and responsibility of the church today, in both its daily administration and its ongoing mission of making disciples of the nations.

Eternal Impact, page 19

The Secret Garden by Frances Hodgson Burnett was first published in 1909. This children's classic, now getting ready to celebrate a century of publication, has been released in book form many times with different illustrators and several times as a movie. The story has mystery, intrigue, suspense, and a key.

Mary, the main character, comes to England to live with her uncle because her parents have died in India. Spending much of her time alone, Mary wanders through the walled gardens of the estate. She notices that there is a large garden she cannot enter. In fact, she cannot even find the door. Eventually she finds both the door to the garden and the key.

When her uncle comes home for a brief visit, Mary asks for "a bit of earth" and for permission to take it from any place "that isn't wanted." With help from other children and a gardener, she transforms the neglected space into a magnificent display of flowers. As winter turns to spring in the garden, Mary's influence also begins to transform the lives of the people around her.

But without access to the garden, no transformation would have taken place. Mary had permission, authority, and the key. The garden, the flowers, and the children's access had been bound (forbidden). Once they were loosed (permitted), change began to take place.

When Christ followers today, members of His established church, take the good news from Jerusalem to the ends of the earth, we do so under Jesus' authority. In fact, that's precisely what He commanded us to do in Matthew 28:19-20 and Acts 1:8.

Can you see some similarities between this children's story and the Gospel message of Matthew 16? Here's one to get you started: The uncle in the story owned the garden; he simply gave his permission for Mary to grow flowers on a bit of earth. Jesus is Lord of the church, but He's given His followers the permission and the responsibility to help it grow, to serve as workers in His kingdom.

Think of a movie or a story where a key is significant—a mysterious key to a treasure box, getting the key to the jail cell from the jailer, "borrowing" the keys to the car. In your story, how does the key have power and authority? Does it always include permission? With the key, what is bound or loosed?

What did the disciples begin to do after receiving Jesus' Great Commission? What was the impact of this small group of disciples?

What is your responsibility as a modern-day disciple? How will you make a difference in the kingdom?

THE COMPREHENSIVE POWER

"Then Jesus came near and said to them, 'All authority has been given to Me in heaven and on earth.'" *Matthew 28:18*

What magnificent potential we have! Hear it again in this well-known benediction: "Now to Him who is able to do exceedingly abundantly above all that we ask or think, according to the power that works in us, to Him be glory in the church by Christ Jesus to all generations, forever and ever. Amen" (Eph. 3:20-21 NKJV).

Eternal Impact, page 31

The Power of One is a movie about a young boy in Africa who wants to change the world. His world of privilege and poverty, the divisions of apartheid, seemed to most to be bigger than any one person's ability to make a difference. Even in the midst of personal tragedy, teenage angst over life and love, peer problems, and school demands, Peekay manages to make a difference in building a better future for Africa.

Most people think they have no power. Many—even Christians—feel more like victims than victorious in their living. They seem to forget that because of their relationship with Jesus Christ they are plugged into the greatest power in the universe—power to make a difference for the kingdom of God.

What keeps people from believing that they, and their church, can make a difference in bringing people to saving faith in Jesus Christ? Perhaps it's a little like the problem my friend had with her cell phone. Out of town on business, she checked into her hotel late one evening after a full day of meetings, negotiation, and a bit of frustration. Unpacking, she took the charger for her phone and plugged it into the wall socket and noted that the light came on, indicating that the charger was receiving electrical power. But when she attached her phone, nothing happened. Futilely she moved the charger from one electrical outlet to another, even though she knew the charger was receiving power. Nothing happened. By the next day the phone had little power left. When she returned home, she went from the airport directly to a phone store, assuming she'd need to purchase a new phone. But when he heard what happened, the store manager deftly removed a tiny piece of tissue that had become lodged in the phone's power port. The only thing wrong with the phone was that something had been blocking the power.

It may not take much, but in many churches and in many Christian's lives, some bit of garbage (sin) may have entered in and is blocking the Power Source. Could that be the case in your church or in your life?

Read Matthew 16:24. What do you think this passage calls you to do? Do you need to deny yourself something? If so, what?

Pray, asking God to point out anything in your life that is interfering with your relationship with Him.

THE UNIVERSAL MISSION

"Go, therefore, and make disciples of all nations, baptizing them in the name of the Father and of the Son and of the Holy Spirit, teaching them to observe everything I have commanded you. And remember, I am with you always, to the end of the age." *Matthew 28:19-20*

Let's head out one more time to the mountaintop summit meeting where the resurrected Lord gave His marching orders to the first-century disciples. From this text we will come face-to-face again with Christ, who alone has the authority to command His church. The questions we must settle in our own hearts while we're there is whether to join His first disciples in the challenge of discipling the nations.

Eternal Impact, pages 32-33

Far from the ideal family, the Simpsons—Homer, Marge, Bart, Lisa, and Maggie—have had TV, and now movie, viewers laughing since 1989. Lisa and Bart are as different as a brother and a sister can be, and they quarrel constantly. Bart is disrespectful of his father, and Homer responds with abuses, both verbal and physical. They face overwhelming situations week after week, but in the end they support one another. Just let an outside force threaten the family and they unite in spite of their differences. They model love and forgiveness and the power of the family.

Is your church anything like the Simpsons? Which is greater -- areas of disagreement that divide the people or a Savior and a mission that unite the church in working together?

Congregations disagree about everything from the color of the carpet to the selection of music for the worship service. And sometimes those disagreements lead to church splits, or disgruntled members feel compelled to find another congregation that better meets their needs. Rather than let internal differences divide them, church members should focus on working together to combat the evil external forces that block reaching people for Christ. Christ followers in a church should be united in fulfilling their church's mission in their own city, and they should be united with other churches to reach a lost world.

Are the forgiveness and love of God and the Gospel of Christ and Jesus' orders to go into all the world unifying forces in your church? In your life?

If someone were to look at your personal budget, schedule, and priorities—your calendar and your checkbook—what would they determine are your priorities?

When you joined the church to which you now belong, what was your first concern? Was it to determine its commitment and strategy for the completion of the Great Commission?

What is your personal involvement in reaching all nations?

Pray that God will give you a passion for joining with others in your congregation to reach the nations with the message of salvation.

FROM JERUSALEM TO THE ENDS OF THE EARTH

Viewer Guide

1. The birth of the church, recorded in the book of Acts, begins with the _____.

2. We _____ witnesses.

3. You are salt and _____.

4. The moment you accept Christ you receive the full expression of God's _____.

5. The filling of the Spirit is the empowering for _____.

6. Church health depends on our _____ to the living Lord.

7. We need to rely on the _____ of the Holy Spirit.t

Notes

FROM JERUSALEM TO THE ENDS OF THE EARTH

What is the greatest distance you have ever traveled from the place where you were born? What was the purpose of your journey? In what ways did you represent Christ during your travels?

Watch this week's DVD.

1. Read Acts 1:3. The "convincing proofs" (NASB) that Jesus is the Messiah, God's only Son are His resurrection appearances. What was the convincing proof that led you to belief in Jesus? How have you shared that convincing proof with others?

2. Read Luke 24:45-47 and Acts 1:4-8. What role did obedience have among Jesus' followers after He was gone? What is the evidence of their obedience? What are the expectations for Christ followers today in obeying God's Word and Jesus' commands? What is the evidence of believers' obedience today?

3. Read Acts 2:1-4. Where were Jesus' followers when they received the power of the Holy Spirit? When has your church experienced the Holy Spirit's power? What happened in individual lives? What happened to the church as a whole?

4. Read Joel 2:27-32 and Acts 2:17. In our post-Pentecost era, the power of God's Holy Spirit is available to all who call Jesus Lord and Savior. Do you see God's power being poured out in the world today? Why or why not?

5. Read Acts 2:32. Peter witnessed Jesus' resurrection. He was there to see the risen Christ. We know this is true from what Peter and the other disciples told us. But we also know because of God's grace and work in our own lives, bringing together what God has done throughout history and what He is doing in our lives today. What is your message, your witness, based on -- historical events when Jesus came to earth, your own salvation experience, and what God is doing in your life today?

Pray that each person present will hear and obey God's call to tell someone about Jesus this week.

THE PROMISE OF THE SPIRIT

"But you will receive power when the Holy Spirit has come upon you, and you will be My witnesses in Jerusalem, in all Judea and Samaria, and to the ends of the earth." *Acts 1:8*

Just as His first-century followers, we too are called to bear witness to Jesus' life-changing power until He returns. We have the same Holy Spirit to empower us that was made available to them. We have the same call to Jerusalem, Judea, Samaria, and the ends of the earth. We have plenty to do, but plenty to do it with. The only question is—will we do it?

Eternal Impact, page 45

Have you noticed how many people are calling themselves *coaches* these days? People who once wore the label *consultant* now pass out business cards with their career changed to *coach*. You can find a coach for business, for fitness, for personal growth and fulfillment, even to get your messy house in order. Some of these are consultants with a new title, still giving advice and telling you what to do. Real coaches help you develop your own plan and take action to move forward in the direction you want to go.

You may be thinking, *If that's all a coach does, then why can't I do what I want to do on my own? Why do I need a coach to help me stay focused and moving forward?* If you're like most people, the reason is that we just don't. Most of us know far more that we ought to do or could do or should do than we actually take action to do.

A coach can help you find your greatest strengths and put them into use. A coach can help you see the world with new insights and from different perspectives. A coach can help you gain new knowledge, to learn and grow.

Many people, including church leaders, have benefited greatly from working with a coach. But you know another place that can help you find, implement, and strengthen gifts; encourage you to be courageous in doing what you are called to do; and continue to grow and learn? It's the church! It's what people in the church ought to be doing—calling out gifts, giving people opportunities to serve, helping them learn and grow, and giving them encouragement to continue putting their faith into action.

When you are empowered by having the Holy Spirit in your life and you are supported by your own congregation, you have every reason to attempt great things for Christ. Will you?

The believer's assignment on this earth is to participate in God's kingdom. What are you doing right now to serve in God's kingdom?

If you could do anything you wanted to do to serve God, what would you do?

What is preventing you from doing this?

What steps can you take right now to serve God in this way?

If you want to learn more about coaching from a kingdom perspective, read Jane Creswell, *Christ-Centered Coaching* (St.. Louis: Chalice Press, 2005).

THE PRIORITY OF PRAYER

"All these were continually united in prayer, along with
the women, including Mary the mother of Jesus,
and His brothers." *Acts 1:14*

Is prayer our first priority, or is it our final recourse? Is
prayer central in all our church meetings? Is prayer our
first thought when it comes to fulfilling the Acts 1:8
challenge? Not just superficial prayer. Not routine prayer.
Not words-with-no-meaning prayer. *Real* prayer.
Eternal Impact, page 46

At one large inner-city church during a recent Sunday morning worship
service—just a typical seventy-five-minute service—at least six prayers
were voiced. They were specific for that day and for that worship service:
a prayer of confession and forgiveness, a prayer for military men and
women, a prayer for church members and their families who were
experiencing grief or illness, a prayer for a children's ministry project, a
prayer during a baby dedication, and the Lord's Prayer. This church was
continually uniting in prayer, and the prayers were voicing the people's
heartfelt needs that Sunday.

Not every worship service in this church includes six prayers, and
the prayers are not always about the same things. But they do pray, pray
together, and pray for one another. They lift up one another's needs when
they are together on Sunday morning and at other times, and they pray
for one another, for the church's leaders, and for the church's mission—
both when they are together and when they are apart. And they are
continually praising God in prayer.

By they way, five people joined that church that day – some by
receiving Christ as Savior and others by moving their membership. The
people in that church expect to see God's hand move like that every
Sunday. Surely the people's prayers make a difference in their fulfilling
Jesus' last command.

In Acts 1 we read that the people did what Jesus told them to do. They prayed, and they waited, and then—after receiving the power of the Holy Spirit—they got busy telling others about Jesus. The acts of praying and waiting don't fit well in our multitasking society today. In one interview about multitasking, a man said that he tried to limit his multitasking to doing five different things at the same time. In our busy world do you take time to pray, to wait on God, to obey His Word, to tell others about Him?

Read Acts 1.
How are prayer, obedience, and results linked?

Is prayer your first step or your last recourse when making a decision? facing a challenge? or just going about your everyday life?

How might your outlook and orientation, as well as outcome and results, change if prayer became more prominent in your life?

PENTECOSTAL POWER

"When the day of Pentecost had arrived,
they were all together in one place." *Acts 2:1*

Pentecost was a community celebration, and so the Jerusalem of Acts 2 was sure to be crowded with Jews and Gentile converts who had come together to celebrate the abundant provision of God.

Eternal Impact, page 52

Many cities and towns these days have a farmers' market where local farmers bring their produce and city dwellers come to buy fresh-from-the-farm vegetables and fruits and sometimes meat and dairy products. That's about as close to the farm as most people get today. They appreciate and enjoy the quality of the fresh food, but they generally have no idea about the labor needed to get the harvest to the people.

In one ex-rural suburb a few older natives still have several acres around their homes, and they plant all their land can hold every year. One woman—a never-married, retired schoolteacher—planted the fields around her house every year with tomatoes, early peas, green beans, butter beans, field peas, onions, corn, peppers, cucumbers, yellow squash, zucchini, watermelons, pumpkins, eggplant, and other vegetables. Later, when these crops had withered, she planted turnip greens. She lived alone, but she planted enough for the entire community. A neighbor helped her prepare the ground. She planted, watered, weeded, and got the garden going every year.

Then she left town. She was a world traveler, and taking care of a garden was not going to slow her down. She partnered with a friend or two to tend the garden and reap the harvest while she was on her extensive "tours," as she called them. The friends dutifully picked vegetables and froze or canned them, sharing them with the owner and others when the landowner returned.

You can draw a lot of biblical parallels from this true story. Let's focus on these:

• Harvest comes only after hard work.
• In the church, as well as in farming, people work together to ensure that harvest comes. Not everyone does the harvesting. Some workers are better skilled at planting the seed and tending the soil.
• When harvest comes, it's time to celebrate and rejoice in seeing the fruit of everyone's labor.

When people in the church work together in the mission God gave them to do, growth will come. The church will grow numerically. People will grow in discipleship and ministry. And as they work together in the kingdom of God, they should rejoice in the privilege to serve in community, and they should celebrate those who enter the kingdom.

Read Luke 24:53; Acts 2:1; 1 Corinthians 12:13; and Acts 1:8.
Early Christ followers came together. What did they do when they were together?

And then they went out to work, going different places, doing kingdom work wherever they went.

What is your role in service through your church and community? How does your work fit into God's kingdom goals? What parts do others play to bring God's plan to fruition?

How does your church celebrate kingdom growth? If they are not currently doing this, how can you begin the celebration?

THE DAYS OF FULFILLMENT AND THE CHURCH

"And it will be in the last days, says God, that I will pour out My Spirit on all humanity." *Acts 2:17*

Are you now manifesting in your life the power of God's Spirit? He has given us His Spirit to enable us to advance His kingdom by serving Him. Are you engaged in kingdom activity through your local church? Think on this: you were created in God's image, redeemed by His grace, empowered and gifted by His Spirit so that you might join Him in kingdom activity until He comes.

Eternal Impact, page 62

He had been a pastor, a Christian university administrator, a husband, a dad. And then he added to that list retiree and later widower. The very words captured the loneliness he felt.

One day he decided he had to get out of the house and be *among* people even if he wasn't really *with* anyone. Surely just having human contact would help. Even the beautiful spring day began to lift his spirits as he got in his car.

But where to go? He'd heard that a nearby theme park was featuring performances by gospel groups that weekend. Maybe that would work. A beautiful spring day. People. And familiar music to praise God. He smiled just thinking about the music of his youth, a change from the choruses he was singing in church these days.

When he got in the park, he got turned around and couldn't locate the area where the performances were scheduled. But he saw a woman with a map and decided to ask for help. And that's how it all began.

Together they located the site on the map. She was going there too. He was a widower. She was a widow. Both were Christians. She'd been praying for God to lead her to such a man. He'd been praying for an end to his loneliness. The more time they spent together, the more interests they discovered they held in common, the more they knew God had brought them together.

God cares about His people one by one and altogether. He hears our cries and heals our hurts. He works in people's lives individually and draws people together to serve in His kingdom's work.

Where have you recently seen God at work in your own life?

Where are you seeing God at work in others' lives?

Where are you seeing God at work in your church?

Where are you seeing God at work in the world?

Read John 16:5-15, 23-33.
What have you asked God to give you recently to enable you to do His kingdom's work?

How will you ask Him to help you join in the work He is doing in your world today?

THE KINGDOM MESSAGE

"Therefore let all the house of Israel know with certainty that
God has made this Jesus, whom you crucified,
both Lord and Messiah!" *Acts 2:36*

Even today, although Jesus hasn't physically walked the
earth for two thousand years, the evidence that testifies
to His life is deep, rich, and historically plentiful. And
the repercussions of His existence, evidence in missions
of followers throughout time and throughout the world
who have continued His kingdom activity, further
cement His authenticity.

Eternal Impact, page 64

In the fall of 2007, the outspoken president of Iran, Mahmoud
Ahmadinejad, visited the United States. Because of his country's links
to terrorism and his citizens' links to the destruction of September
11, 2001, his visit was tightly controlled. He was not allowed to visit
Ground Zero in New York where the twin towers of the World Trade
Center once stood. But during his visit, he spoke at Columbia University,
causing much controversy. Many of his remarks seem strange to our ears,
including his denial of the Jewish holocaust during World War II. He
says it's a matter of opinion, not historical fact. But his adamant stance
does not erase the eradication of six million Jews under Hitler's rule of
Nazi Germany.

Do Iranians believe their leader? Do they also think the
holocaust is a myth? Or, to protect themselves, do they just
ignore the evidence and choose not to confront their president?
If Ahmadinejad surrounds himself by people who give lip service
to support his belief that the holocaust did not occur, does that change
the truth?

God has acted throughout history. Those who believe and watch for
God at work in the world consistently see His mighty deeds, His personal
touch, His saving power. In Acts 2, Peter preached with excitement
because he knew that Jesus lives, that He was resurrected from the dead,

that He came to seek and to save all of us, and that He alone gives power to do God's kingdom work. He wasn't telling something he had simply read in a history book. Peter told what he knew and what he personally had experienced.

Unfortunately today, many do not believe that God continues to act in miraculous ways. They often attribute the works of God to luck or chance or to something people do in their own strength. But the fact that they don't believe does not change God's work in the world today.

Jesus' last command was to be His witnesses wherever we go. We can tell the historical good news—that Jesus came and taught and died and rose again to give those who believe eternal life with Him. But we should also be giving witness to what God is doing right now—in our own lives, in the life of our church, and throughout the world.

Is your witness about Jesus limited to what He did on earth?
Or does it also include what He's doing in your life today?

Why is it important to tell about how God is at work today and not just in the past?

At a trial, not all witnesses say the same thing because each witness has a slightly different perspective. What is your unique witness for Christ based on what He has done in your life?

When did you last tell someone about your relationship with Christ?

Watch to see where God is at work in your world, and tell somebody about it!

Viewer Guide

1. A church with the right _____ will discover the right methodology.

2. Methodology changes; _____ is the same.

3. God measures the _____.

4. God's heartbeat is that everyone would come to know Him as _____.

5. Character Trait 1—United in _____

6. Character Trait 2—Sound _____

7. Character Trait 3—_____ to the Ends of the Earth

8. Character Trait 4—Intentional _____

9. Evangelism is intentional and _____.

10. Every church needs a strategy for _____.

3

Notes

FROM CHARACTER TO FUNCTION

The Eight Character Traits of the Kingdom-Centered Church, Part 1

Does character matter in the world today? What evidence do you see that character does or does not matter?

In our lesson today we will look at the early church's character and those character traits that God desires churches to have today.

Watch this week's DVD.

1. Read Acts 2:41-42. God's power and the people's prayers are linked together throughout the book of Acts.

Read Acts 6:1-6. What were the reasons for enlisting deacons? Apparently the apostles were both praying and leading the church in prayer. Do your leaders spend more time in ministry or in preaching and in prayer?

How would you describe your church's prayer life? How would you describe the way God is working in your church right now?

2. Read Acts 9:31. What were the characteristics of the early church?

What characteristics does your church have? Thank God for all the gifts He has given your church. Pray for His help in overcoming any undesirable characteristics.

3. Read Acts 11:26. This verse links intensive study with those who are called Christians. What are the strong points of your church's Bible and doctrine teaching ministry? How could it improve? How can your church get more people involved in studying God's Word and learning sound doctrine?

4. Read Acts 2:46-47. Worship wasn't a one-hour, once-a-week event for people in the early church. It was a part of who they were, of what they did each day.

How important is worship in your life? in the life of your church? What can your church do to teach people the importance of worship? What can you do to ensure that people connect with God when they come to your worship services?

5. Read Acts 4:8. What were the circumstances for Peter's preaching? In the early church the spread of the Gospel was accompanied by opposition, imprisonment, persecution, and even death? Have you ever suffered because you told others about Jesus? What keeps more people from telling others the good news? Whom will you tell this week?

Pray that Christians will obey God's Word and show God's love in all their dealings with others this week.

If you desire to learn how Jesus demonstrated the Gospel, see splashinfo.com. Consider this six–week Bible study as a next step in living with Eternal Impact.

CHARACTERISTIC 1—UNITED IN PRAYER AND EMPOWERED BY THE SPIRIT

"And they devoted themselves to the apostle's teaching, to fellowship, to the breaking of bread, and to prayers. Then fear came over everyone, and many wonders and signs were being performed through the apostles." *Acts 2:42-43*

Prayer and the empowering of the Spirit are interrelated. Therefore, when we think of them in the context of a kingdom-centered church, we should consider them a single characteristic, foundational for everything else. Prayer is the key to supernatural empowering. If you have one, you have the other.

Eternal Impact, page 73

A young woman found herself on a long flight seated next to a Korean pastor. She'd heard about the growth of Christianity in Korea, and she enjoyed talking about their mutual love for Jesus and about the exciting ministries in their churches. When they reached their destination and began to say their good-byes, the pastor suggested that they agree to pray for each other fifteen minutes every day for the next year. In the hurry of the moment and the enthusiasm of the time they had shared, she said yes. She quickly learned, as she began to fulfill her promise, that the Korean Christian's concept of prayer was very different from most Americans. Few Americans pray fifteen minutes a week, much less fifteen minutes a day for one person for a full year.

Churches today often have a prayer team. One person takes prayer concerns from the Internet and prays for that concern. Perhaps one person receives and distributes e-mail messages with prayer concerns. Occasionally word goes out and many people pray as a response to an accident, an illness, or a death. Seldom does the church come together for the purpose of praying for the church.

Have you ever been in a church that had a round-the-clock prayer vigil? Not many churches do this today, but in the past churches would plan for one or two people to come every hour to pray around the clock for a church revival or another concern. Yet when Peter was jailed, the church was together praying for him in the middle of the night. Their prayer was answered; and Peter, released from jail, apparently knew just where to go—to the home of Mary, mother of John Mark, where the people were praying.

What evidence do you see in the book of Acts that prayer was important in the early church? Read, for example, Acts 12:5-11; 13:2-3; 20:36; 21:5-6.

What evidence do you see of God's power? Read, for example, Acts 2:41-42.

When have you prayed and then seen God's power at work in your own life? in the life of someone for whom you prayed? in the life of your church?

Try praying fifteen minutes a day this week. Here are some kingdom concerns to help you create your own list.

1. Pray for those in authority in all realms of society with the specific concern that the Gospel will continue to spread.
2. Pray for boldness and safety for persons who are sharing the Gospel in all four quadrants of the Acts 1:8 imperative.
3. Pray for unsaved persons by name.
4. Pray that church members will come to appropriate the full resources available to them.
5. Pray that every church member will walk worthy of their calling and that the spirit of unity will be enriched.
6. Ask the Lord of the harvest to compel laborers to go into the ripe fields.
7. Pray for specific ministry needs of the church.

UNITED IN PRAYER AND EMPOWERED BY THE SPIRIT, PART 2

"So the church throughout all Judea, Galilee, and Samaria
had peace, being built up and walking in the fear of the Lord
and in the encouragement of the Holy Spirit,
and it increased in numbers. *Acts 9:31*

In our desire to see our church grow and advance
God's kingdom, we are often tempted to rely upon
new methods, strategies, and structures. But whenever
we depend on anything other than the Spirit to grow
our church, we run the risk of making an idol of
church growth methodology. Honestly, if a plan or
program could grow our church, we would depend
on it rather than God. He knows it. And we know it.

Eternal Impact, page 81

Santa Fe, New Mexico is filled with art galleries. Going from one
to another and seeing what creative artists have displayed is always
interesting. One gallery had a number of large sculptures. Among
them was a life-size likeness of a well-chiseled man from the waist up.
In one hand he held a mallet, and in the other hand he held a chisel.
The humorous title of this statue was "Self-made Man." The artist had
caught the contemporary irony of anyone's thinking that his success is
due entirely to his own ability and hard work. Yet most people in today's
society live as if they created themselves from nothing and deserve every
good thing that comes their way. When misfortune comes, however,
those same people are not so eager to take the blame. Taking credit
comes much easier for them.

Have you ever seen those TV features with interviews of people
who have reached or passed the age of one hundred? The decagenarians
are always asked why they think they have lived so long. Occasionally
someone will say they are alive by the grace of God, but more often they
take the credit for their long lives based on what they eat or drink or do
each day. I've never heard one say that they are alive because they are

blessed to live in a place and an age with better health care. They seem to be convinced that they are alive because of what they have or have not done. Much like the self-made man.

Are we so different in the church today? A growing church offers clinics to show others how to do what they have done. A church that has plateaued or is declining rarely examines its own prayer life or relationship with God.

Giving God all the glory for health and growth, both personally and in the church, may sound too simple for some people. Yet no answer is more true, more mysterious, or more wonderful. All that we have comes from God, and every day we live by His power.

Paul called the attitude that we can be anything apart from God carnality. Read Romans 7:14; 8:6-7.

When have you taken credit for something you have done, knowing that God gave you the gifts and talents and health to do the job? He may also have given you the ideas, opened doors for you, prepared those with whom you worked so that you might succeed.

Recall a recent success in your life. List all the ways that success was a result of God's provision. Now thank God for what He has done in your life.

Make a list of ways God has blessed your church. Thank Him for each one.

CHARACTERISTIC 2—
FOUNDED ON SOUND DOCTRINE

"And they devoted themselves to the apostles' teaching." *Acts 2:42*

Knowing and being able to articulate one's beliefs was crucial to the life of the early church. When we read about Paul and Barnabas's work with the believers in Antioch, we are told, "For a whole year they met with the church and taught large numbers, and the disciples were first called Christians in Antioch" (Acts 11:26). Thorough training was not an option for the early church but was done with much care and concern for their doctrinal integrity. In fact, this was championed to such a degree that the believers in Antioch began being referred to as Christians—"little Christs" or "imitators of Christ"— after this intensive time of theological instruction. "The apostles' teaching" had led to life transformation. It still does.   *Eternal Impact*, page 88

Recall the story of Priscilla and Aquila. Paul met them in Corinth. Priscilla and Aquila had come to Corinth from Rome because Emperor Claudius had made all the Jews leave Rome. Paul went to visit them.

Have you ever wondered why he went to see them? Did he go because he heard there were new tent makers in town? Did he go because he wanted to ask about the dangers for Christians in Rome? Or did he go because he heard there were new folks in town and he wanted to tell them about Jesus? We don't know. We don't know whether they were already Christians or became Christians after meeting Paul.

But we do know that they became good friends and even lived together, making tents side by side. At the same time the Bible says that Paul was teaching in the synagogue every week and trying to persuade both Jews and Greeks to become Christians. Can't you see them passing the hours making their tents and talking about Jesus at the same time? Aquila and Priscilla probably also heard Paul teach in the synagogue week after week.

When Paul decided to leave Corinth and sail to Syria, Priscilla and Aquila went with him. When they came to Ephesus, Paul taught in the synagogue and then left Aquila and Priscilla there while he continued his journey.

A Jew named Apollos came to Ephesus and began to speak in the synagogue about Jesus. He spoke well, but his information was incomplete. When Aquila and Priscilla heard him, they saw how gifted he was as a powerful speaker and they saw that he believed in Jesus. They invited him into their home, taught him more accurately, and sent him on his way to tell the good news in other places.

People from other countries who desire to become a citizen must take a test on American history and government. Frequently, when asked the same questions, people born in the United States are unable to answer correctly. In the same way, many people today, both inside and outside the church, seem to know little about what the Bible says much less about theology or doctrine. If you had to take a test to be a kingdom citizen, how well would you do?

Do you regularly (daily) read the Bible?

Do you participate in group Bible study?

Do you encourage and teach others who need to grow in their understanding of God's Word?

What steps will you take to continue your own personal growth and to ensure that the next generation is equipped with sound doctrine?

CHARACTERISTIC 3—WORSHIPPING TO THE ENDS OF THE EARTH

"Let the peoples praise You, God,
let all the peoples praise You." *Psalm 67:5*

Worship is central to the kingdom-centered church, not because it suits the tastes of its participants, but because it flows out of devotion to the King and provides the passion and power that cause the church to extend its ministry to the ends of the earth. Worship should cause us to focus our attention on God, who alone is worthy of praise and worship. And like everything else we do, it should keep us passionate about reaching the peoples and nations of the world so that they too will know and worship Him.

Eternal Impact, page 94

A friend told this story about her trip to Russia.

In 1998, communism had fallen and churches were once again opening their doors to worship. I was there with my husband who was part of a singing group. Since they spent so much time in rehearsal, the few of us who were not singing had time to do some things on our own. We were there during the Feast of the Holy Trinity in the Russian Orthodox Church. This meant there were frequent services throughout the week.

One night before a performance, I wandered into a nearby church during a worship service. Although I couldn't understand a word, I saw the people praying, singing, and hearing God's Word. They were completely captivated by every moment of worship, hungry for it. I stayed, observing, worshipping with them, for about twenty minutes. I don't know how long their service lasted, but they stood the entire time. There were no chairs or benches or pews. They stood to worship God.

The next day three of us took off to a monastery outside Moscow. Our transportation was provided by a man who spoke no English; and we, of course, spoke no Russian—not a word. We faced some communication challenges that day, but some things need no words.

On the trip words were few. The three Americans were busy taking in the scenery. As we neared the monastery, we saw people walking in the direction we were going. Many people were going to the monastery because of the feast days. A mile or so away I saw an old man on crutches moving painfully along the sidewalk, though I thought little about it—just part of seeing all the people and buildings as the traffic slowed.

We spent a couple of hours seeing the buildings and grounds of the monastery. As we left to try to find our driver among the hundreds of cars crowded around the monastery, I spotted the crippled man. He had finally reached the gate to the monastery. The man had been on his way to worship all along.

I remembered with shame the weeks I had spent on crutches, most of the time not going to church because moving around was so difficult—just getting in and out of the car, not walking for miles.

What price would you pay to worship with other Christ followers in your church?

Read Romans 12:1. Paul indicates that worship involves our total being. What does that mean to you?

How does your relationship with God affect how you live each day?

What goals do you have for making worship reflect your love for God—heart, soul, mind, and strength—every day in every part of your life?

CHARACTERISTIC 4— INTENTIONALLY EVANGELISTIC

"But you will receive power when the Holy Spirit has come upon you, and you will be My witnesses in Jerusalem, in all Judea and Samaria, and to the ends of the earth." *Acts 1:8*

The book of Acts is largely an example God's people responding to the opportunities He had placed before them. The early disciples simply entered each day expecting to be part of God's kingdom agenda. And as the Spirit made them aware of what was happening, they trusted Him to provide them with the right words, the right timing, the right sensitivity to what needed doing.

Eternal Impact, page 103

Here's a story from a friend about ends-of-the-earth witnessing.

We'd walked for hours down dusty roads in a suburb of Buenos Aires. In this area some houses were simple, some were nicer with walls and gates, and between the houses were small industries and empty lots used as soccer fields. This area clearly knew nothing of the zoning laws that group businesses and houses.

The temperature was above 105°. We were hot, tired, and thirsty. And although people had been kind and friendly, no one that day had made a decision to accept Christ.

We had a set time to get back to the church to prepare for evening worship, and that time was getting close. We decided to head in that direction. One of the three in our group said, "Let's just try one more house." It was walled and gated, so we rang the doorbell at the gate. We waited. We buzzed again. We waited. Finally the door opened and a petite middle-aged woman came to the gate. We told her who we were, and she responded, "God has sent you to me today. Come in."

Her name was Mercedes, but her circumstances were inconsistent with the wealth her name implied. She shared her story. Both she and her husband had lost their jobs. She was completely out of money and wondering what she would feed her family that night—her husband and young grandson. She had contemplated suicide, but out of concern for her grandson, she was looking for a way out of her difficulty. She had found her Bible and tried to read it, but she had broken her glasses and could not see well enough to read it.

We asked for permission to tell her the good news of the Bible. While our Spanish-speaking team member shared the Gospel, the other two team members prayed. The woman accepted Christ and promised to come to church that night, including the meal before the worship service.

We hurried to the church, so happy that Mercedes had accepted Christ as Savior. But on the inside I was still troubled about all that she faced. How would her newfound belief solve her hunger?

When Mercedes arrived a few minutes later, I didn't recognize her. She looked ten years younger, like a burden had been lifted. As people rejoiced with her, other things began to happen in this small church with limited means. Our team had resources to take her to a nearby grocery to provide food for the next few days. A hairdresser offered free haircuts for her and her grandson (I thought he was a girl when I first saw him.), and another said she knew a pharmacist who had connections to get her free glasses. Someone else knew about a temporary job. One by one this small community of faith met her needs—both spiritual and physical.

I looked on in wonder, thinking that the early church must have been a lot like this.

Which of Mercedes' needs was greater, her need for Christ or her physical needs?

Which type of needs are many Christians more willing to supply?

What are the benefits of helping people both spiritually and physically?

How can you make sure you always share the good news when you have opportunities to help meet people's physical needs?

Viewer Guide

1. Character Trait 5—_____

2. Character Trait 6—Generous Stewardship

3. Character Trait 7—Global in Its _____

4. Character Trait 8—_____

5. The church has one _____.

6. The church needs to move beyond church _____ to kingdom expansion.

7. The church's concern is to develop fully formed _____ of Christ.

4

Notes

FROM CHARACTER TO FUNCTION

The Eight Character Traits of the Kingdom-Centered Church, Part 2

In daily life, which character trait is most important to you? Why? Which character traits of the church that we've studied so far is most important to you? Why?

In our lesson today we will continue to look at the early church's character and those character traits that God desires churches to have today.

Watch this week's DVD.

1. Read John 13:34-35; 15:12, 17; 1 Corinthians 1:9.

With whom are Christians to find fellowship?

Why is fellowship with both God and other believers essential?

How does your church practice Christian fellowship?

2. Read Acts 4:32-37. How would you describe stewardship among members of the early church?

How would you describe stewardship among members of your church?

Why is stewardship an important church characteristic?

3. Read Acts 1:8; 13:1-3. The early church had a fourfold strategy—pray, go, send, and give—to reach the nations with the good news of salvation through Jesus Christ. How does your church engage in each of these four functions?

4. Read Acts 11:27-30. This example shows how the early churches collected money for a need greater than any individual or small group could meet alone.

What are some ways your church cooperates with other churches to meet needs? Include both giving and doing ministry.

5. Read Acts 11:26. In this passage how were the church leaders fulfilling the Great Commission? How is your church growing disciples? How does this relate to your church's fulfilling the Great Commission?

Read Galatians 5:22-25. Pray that these characteristics will be seen in the lives of those present in all their relationships this week.

CHARACTERISTIC 5—
NURTURING BIBLICAL FELLOWSHIP

"And they devoted themselves ... to fellowship." *Acts 2:42*

When we meet the needs of others, we discover that the Spirit ministers to us. We become the kind of church where newcomers and long-timers, new believers and mature saints, young and old share a common bond of fellowship.

Eternal Impact, page 109

James and Terri had served in various church staff roles most of their adult life. One or the other of them had served as pianist, organist, minister of education, or youth pastor for many years. Having that role in church had kept them busy, involved in a church, and happy serving the Lord.

Then they moved. With job pressures, including a good bit of traveling, they decided to find a church where both would be happy serving in ways their busy professional schedules allowed—just not as paid staff.

Finding a church was difficult. Perhaps it was because it had been so many years since they had actually looked for a church. For many years they had been chosen to serve a church; they had not been looking for a church. They learned that choosing a church was different from being called to one.

Finally they agreed on a church. It was much larger than any of the churches they had served, but there were a lot of people their age, and they felt certain they'd soon be busy and connected. But that just didn't happen.

People rarely spoke to them on Sunday morning.

Sunday School was a little more friendly but formal. People nodded sometimes.

One Sunday night, soon after they had joined the church, they went to a special gospel singing event. When they walked into fellowship hall, they found that it was already really crowded. As they looked around for a place to sit, someone they had met in Sunday School shouted, "Don't you know you need to get here early to find a seat?" Finally they found two chairs together in a corner. After the singing, there was an ice cream party outdoors. There were many people there, a few they had met. People sat in chairs at tables or on benches at picnic tables. When they looked for a seat, no one at a table invited them to join their group.

They began to ask people to go out to lunch after church. One other couple went out with them once. Others had routines, going out with family or the same friends.

Over time and wondering why they weren't making friends more quickly, they began to observe half-century celebrations for people who had reached their 50th birthday and had been in the church all their lives. There seemed to be a lot of those. They heard people talk about having been friends since elementary school. They realized that most of the church members had all the relationships they needed and weren't looking for new ones.

Terri and James wondered if they had been wrong in choosing this church. After spending their entire lives in church, they couldn't figure out how to get involved. After much discussion, James made an appointment to talk with the pastor to get his ideas about getting involved. The pastor told James that the areas where James and Terri felt they had gifts were not his responsibility. They could talk with one of the other staff ministers.

James and Terri decided to look for another church.

This story of a couple seeking fellowship in a church is a sad tale. But even sadder is that they are not alone in their loneliness. Such situations happen often in our churches today. Could any of these events have happened in your church?

Read Acts 2:46. In what ways is this verse a model for church fellowship today?

When have you experienced real fellowship with others in your church? How did that fellowship make you feel?

How can you ensure that others in your church, both newcomers and those who may still be looking for a way to connect, find true fellowship in your church?

CHARACTERISTIC 6— GENEROUS IN STEWARDSHIP

"Now the multitude of those who believed were of one heart and soul, and no one said that any of his possessions was his own, but instead they held everything in common." *Acts 4:32*

If we expect to see local and global impact for the gospel in our current day, it too will come at the cost of our precious love for our prized possessions. We need to take a lesson from the first-century church and practice generous stewardship.

Eternal Impact, pages 116–17

As he drove to work that morning, Jerry thought, as he sat in a line of traffic, how much his part of town had changed. He had moved to the almost rural area twenty-seven years ago with his wife and kids, he'd done so to take a part-time job on a church staff. That had ended long ago, but he and his family loved the area and decided to stay. The school system was good with its small-town atmosphere but bigger city opportunities.

But in recent years the area had really changed. Houses were getting larger and lots were getting smaller. In fact, he and his wife drove over to look at a new subdivision just a couple of miles away where the houses were selling for well over a million dollars. And new communities seemed to be popping up every week. Could the city's suburbs really have taken over their quiet community?

They'd also noticed that the people moving in were a little different. When he'd served on the church staff, money really wasn't an issue. People gave generously. When he noticed all the big new homes, their lavish landscaping and backyard pools, and the three-car garages with at least two SUVs at every house, he thought, *No wonder giving is down at church. Some of these people must be stretched to keep up with their expensive lifestyles.*

What could he do? he wondered. He'd never even thought about tithing before. He just did it. Special offerings too. He loved to give to his church and to help those in need. Perhaps he and his wife needed to look again at their budget to see if they could dig a little deeper. After all, they were content, and contentment kept them from overspending.

He had to laugh out loud alone in the car. Here he was in his ten-year-old Camry with a dented fender. Sometimes his family thought he was a little too content.

Then he saw it, the vanity plate on the car that he had just let in from a side street. The Mercedes's plate read: IGOTMIN. I got mine.

And that's what's happened to our community, he realized. The new folks moving in are not interested in giving to the church, helping the schools, getting involved with local charities. They're focused on one thing—taking care of themselves.

Now he began to think even more about his church. For him to increase his giving wasn't the answer. His church had to find a way to teach people in the church, and perhaps even in the community, about the real joy of giving. Before the week ended, he promised himself that he'd meet with his pastor and begin to look for ideas to help the church by teaching about the benefits of stewardship. He was determined to make a difference—and maybe even find that guy in the Mercedes and lead him to a new understanding!

Read Deuteronomy 15:7. Is your own practice of giving consistent with this verse?

Read Malachi 3:7-10. Is your worship consistent with this teaching from Malachi?

Has God poured out His blessings on you? How have you responded in returning to Him a portion of what He has given you?

Do you need to set new stewardship guidelines for you and your family? What goals will you set?

For more on developing an understanding and practice of Christian stewardship, see Ken Hemphill's *Making Change*.

CHARACTERISTIC 7—
GLOBAL IN ITS MISSION

"But you will receive power when the Holy Spirit has come upon you, and you will be My witnesses in Jerusalem, in all Judea and Samaria, and to the ends of the earth." *Acts 1:8*

> Do you believe your church has the potential to advance the kingdom to the ends of the earth? No matter where your church is located and no matter what its relative size, your church has both the commission and the empowering to "disciple the nations." The Great Commission and the accompanying Acts 1:8 challenge is the primary task of your church. Have you ever thought your church could have a global impact?
>
> *Eternal Impact*, page 124

The little church was comprised primarily of well-educated professional people—self-employed professionals, business owners, educators, doctors, lawyers, people who worked in nonprofit organizations, and retired professionals. Some of them earned more than the average for their community. Others, though well-educated, had chosen to work in jobs that let them serve rather than jobs that made them rich. It was a congregation that took seriously Jesus' command to take up their cross and follow Him daily.

Every year when the church formed its budget, members expected lively debate. Everyone had local, national, and international missions and ministries that they wanted to include. And the church just didn't have enough money to fund all the causes they cared about. They consistently gave their time; they wanted their church to give money too. Always in the budget, after denominational giving, were the soup kitchen, Room in the Inn, Habitat for Humanity, and the mission they supported in Cuba— places where members spent their time as well as their money. No one disagreed about these. It was all the others they wanted to add every year that drew the discussion.

And every year the church struggled financially. They neglected their building; they didn't want to spend money there. They rarely used church funds for fellowship or other expenditures. They had plenty of fellowship times; they just usually found other ways to pay for them.

The percentage of money they gave to missions and ministries kept growing—10 percent, then 11, 12, 13 percent. But they didn't always have all the missions money every month. Usually it balanced over the year, but month by month it was sometimes a struggle. The people gave consistently of what they earned; most of them didn't have a salaried job, so their income varied from month to month.

Finally one of the financial professionals in the church came up with a plan. He talked with a local bank and arranged a line of credit to smooth out the highs and lows of the church budget from month to month. That way the church could always meet its missions giving goals every month, even if the funds were not available in the church's checking account.

Some were skeptical. But it worked. The church kept giving to missions, growing in their giving. And they continued their lively annual debates about all the ministries they wanted to support.

This church was active in giving and going, praying and sending others to tell the Gospel around the world. How are you engaged in your church's fourfold strategy to reach the world for Christ—to pray, go, send, and give—the strategy developed in the early church at Antioch?

• Praying

• Going

• Sending

• Giving

Write a prayer asking God to direct you in your personal strategy to reach the nations.

CHARACTERISTIC 8—WORKING COOPERATIVELY FOR KINGDOM ADVANCEMENT

"Everyone should look out not only for his own interests, but also for the interests of others." Philippians 2:4

God has designed every church—whatever its size or location—to work in cooperation with other churches for kingdom expansion. All are equal partners.

No single church working alone can reach its own local community, much less advance the kingdom to the ends of the earth. When churches work cooperatively, their strength is multiplied and magnified.

Eternal Impact, pages 131–32

Here's the story of Faith Baptist Church. Faith is a relatively new church in a small town in the Midwest. It's a fictitious church, but its story could be yours.

The church leadership team of Faith Baptist Church met for annual planning. They dreamed of what they would like to do in the coming year.

The Sunday School director wanted the church to offer Vacation Bible School for the children in the community. No other church in the area provided VBS. The children had never experienced this important part of childhood.

Another leader wanted to provide a ministry for the transients who came through town as well as residents who sometimes needed help. The town needed a ministry that provided food, clothing, and financial assistance for medical and utility bills.

The church leaders were perplexed. They wanted to carry out both of these ministries, but they knew their resources were limited. They agreed to pray about these concerns, look for options, and meet again in a month.

At work one day the Sunday School leader shared her vision for a VBS with a coworker who also had fond memories of VBS when she was a child. She told her husband. He told a friend. Before the month was out, the Sunday School leader was working with two other churches to come together to provide a VBS in the community. By working together, they had enough leaders to run VBS and enough money to buy all the needed resources.

A similar solution resulted for the benevolent ministry. By partnering together, several churches were able to do what one church alone could not do. And as a result of these initial partnering projects, Faith strengthened its community ties, its stewardship of resources, and its kingdom impact. The church began to look for other ways to cooperate. They participated in a multicultural, multiethnic Christian Thanksgiving service. They opened their doors to host a community arts fair. And their cooperation brought in many people who had never heard of the new church. Some drove past it every day without noticing it. Now the church's name seemed to be everywhere.

Now Faith looked for ways to cooperate with other churches. They partnered with a Baptist church in a nearby town to plan a retreat for both churches' teenagers. This led to a summer missions trip for these students, which led to stronger student disciples and a growing witness on the school campus.

Faith found that cooperation was one of their favorite words. Working with others was a great way to do kingdom work, to be good stewards of their limited resources, to find fellowship with other believers, to support one another in times of need, and most of all, to spread the good news of Jesus Christ to more people in more places.

Read Acts 20:32-35. Paul shares his own belief about supporting himself while providing for others. What needs make you want to give?

When have you experienced the joy of giving, along with others, to meet a need you could not meet alone?

How can you communicate that joy to others?

THE UNIFYING PURPOSE— DISCIPLE THE NATIONS

"All authority has been given to Me in heaven and on earth.
Go, therefore, and make disciples of all nations." *Matthew 28:18-19*

If we are going to be effective at the task of disciple-making, we must first have some idea of what it means to be disciples…

If we are going to produce disciples that are effective instruments through whom the King can advance His kingdom to the ends of the earth, we must be willing to devote the time and energy it takes to produce disciples.

Eternal Impact, page 149

This week's news is not much different from any recent week:

• Two service station managers got in an argument because one of them lowered his prices. The competitor, in anger, shot him. He was not disciplined to deal with his anger in an acceptable way.

• The housing market is in trouble because people purchased homes they could not afford. They were not disciplined in their spending.

• Athletes are being investigated for using steroids. They took shortcuts in their training rather then discipline themselves through hard work.

• More and more people are overweight due to undisciplined eating and exercise habits.

• Lotteries are thriving because people want to get rich without having the discipline to work and save and curtail their spending so that they can increase their net worth.

• Abortions, also a result of lack of discipline, are a national disgrace.

In many areas of life today, people—from young to old, children and adults—lack discipline. They want to take the easy way but reap all the benefits of a disciplined life.

To be a disciple requires discipline—training, commitment, sticking with your objective even when it's difficult.

Following Christ, trying to live your life according to His example, is no easy task. It's a lifelong commitment that requires a disciplined life.

Personal trainers, in trying to change people's eating and exercise habits, say that if a person can maintain a healthy habit for six weeks to two months, the habit is more likely to become a part of routine living. The eight character traits of the early church apply to individual members as well as to the church. We've found in our study that each of the character traits is something the early church practiced repeatedly, not just once and not randomly. They consistently were known for these eight characteristics. The people:

1. Were united in prayer and empowered by the Spirit
2. Taught sound doctrine
3. Worshipped to the ends of the earth
4. Were intentionally evangelistic
5. Nurtured biblical fellowship
6. Practiced generous stewardship
7. Developed a global missions strategy
8. Worked cooperatively for kingdom advancement

The people were disciplined and they grew as disciples. What's more they helped others grow as disciples. They taught, trained, preached, and encouraged. Sometimes the apostles and missionaries and others stayed at a place for a period of time, teaching and equipping. But they were not deserted. Paul sent people in his place with greetings and instructions, and he wrote letters to instruct, correct, and encourage people in their daily walk with Christ.

It's time for mature disciples to move from growing to helping others grow. Only by continuing to make disciples of each generation will God's good news reach all the nations and people of the earth.

What practices in your life indicate that you are a disciplined person?

Which of the character traits are most evident in your life?

How are you continuing to grow while helping others to grow as disciples?

What goals do you have for continued growth?

FROM CHARACTER TO FUNCTION

The Eight Character Traits of the Kingdom-Centered Church, Part 2

Viewer Guide

1. Christ ought to be in charge of the _____.

2. Three Pastoral Tasks

   To _____ among, give pastoral care

   To have _____ over

   To give _____, to equip the saints

3. I can serve the _____.

4. Five Ways We Sacrifice

   Our _____

   Our _____

   Our _____

   Our Good _____

   Our _____

5. You've been _____ by the Spirit of God.

6. God gifts the church in every _____ to accomplish His mission task.

7. God uses gifted _____ like you to accomplish His task.

Notes

FROM LEADERSHIP
TO GIFTED MEMBERSHIP

Think of a time when you and/or your family received ministry from a pastor, another minister, a deacon, or a church member. What did receiving ministry mean to you?

Think of a time when you ministered to someone else. What did this opportunity to serve mean to you?

Watch this week's DVD.

1. Read Galatians 6:1-6 and 1 Thessalonians 5:12-14. List the duties of these early Christian leaders. How do these responsibilities compare to what pastors and other ministers do today?

2. Read Acts 6:1-7. What roles do deacons in your church play? Do their roles match the model in Acts 6?

3. Read Exodus 19:3-6 and 1 Peter 2:9. What does God promise His people? What does God expect from His people?

4. Read Romans 12:6-8; 1 Corinthians 12:4-11. Who has spiritual gifts? How did they get them? How should people use their spiritual gifts?

5. Read Ephesians 4:11-12 and Hebrews 13:20-21. How are people equipped to serve in your church? How does this "equipping" enable people to do more of the church's work? How does equipping lead to the church's fulfilling its mission?

Pray for church leaders by name and by need.

LEADERSHIP FOR THE KINGDOM-CENTERED COMMUNITY

"When they had appointed elders in every church and prayed with fasting, they committed them to the Lord in whom they had believed." Acts 14:23

At this point the church was not as concerned about titles as about structure and function. They knew one thing and they knew it well: spiritual leadership was essential for the health and growth of the kingdom-centered church. It still is. *Eternal Impact*, page 146

Everybody loved Pastor Jim. Almost from the day he moved into the community and assumed his pastoral role in his new church field, he was out in the businesses of the small town and in people's homes, making friends, developing relationships, and leading people to Christ. He was equally comfortable sitting on a hay bale in the feed store, drinking coffee at Starbucks with his student pastor, or repairing the plumbing at the widow's house down the street.

He was a good listener. Whether counseling a family with an unmarried daughter and an unplanned pregnancy, helping a staff minister with a relationship issue, or visiting a new business owner, he listened more than he talked. He never needed to be the center of attention.

Although he was the pastor, he was more than willing for others to lead their areas of responsibility. He had plenty of leadership ability, but he equipped others to grow in using their gifts rather than having a take-charge, tell-others-what-to-do attitude. When he gave advice, people listened because they knew his words were well chosen and kind.

Some said he was more a preacher than a pastor; others said he needed to take more of a leadership role. But others said just the opposite. He tended to take on the role that was needed at the time. He had a vision for the church, and he was enthusiastic about it. People gladly got on board with him and joined him in fulfilling the church's mission.

The biggest criticism he ever got was when a small group of malcontents complained that the church was growing too fast. Afraid they would lose their little bit of influence and control, they tried to convince others that double-digit additions each Sunday was more than the church could handle. Few listened to such ridiculous whining.

Pastor Jim has moved now from kingdom ministry to living with the King. But he's left a legacy in that community that continues to draw people to Christ.

Pastor Jim took on the biblical aspects of church leadership. Read 1 Thessalonians 5:12-14 and Galatians 6:1-6. In what ways did Pastor Jim fulfill the leadership models of the early church?

Although the pastor is the head of the church, all Christians are called to minister. You can join your pastor in pastoral care. Using your gifts, how can you help others in need?

You can benefit from the leadership of your pastor and others by equipping yourself for greater service. How are you growing in your ability to reach and serve others?

One of the pastor's roles is instruction. But the pastor can't teach everyone. Not everyone is called to teach, but all Christians can take a role in growing disciples. How are you helping others learn and grow?

A pastor should love his people. How do your words in and about your church spread peace and love?

A GROWING CHURCH ELECTS DEACONS

"It would not be right for us to give up preaching about God to wait on tables. Therefore, brothers, select from among you seven men of good reputation, full of the Spirit and wisdom, whom we can appoint to this duty." Acts 6:2-3

The English word deacon is virtually a transliteration of the Greek noun *diakonos*.... In secular Greek usage, the word diakonos often was used to convey something of an inferior status. This makes the New Testament choice of this term even more significant. Could it be that this specific word was selected for these early growth ministers because of Jesus' emphasis on greatness through servanthood? Thus the diaconate ministry is patterned after the servant spirit of our Lord, who measures greatness not in fame and recognition but in faithful obedience to whatever a person has been called to do, no matter how seemingly small or insignificant.

Eternal Impact, page 154

Dale has moved more people than some small moving companies. He's a deacon in a church that has lots of young adults in it—and a few older adults too—and they always seem to be on the move. He's not as young as he once was although he still keeps up with his largely younger crew. But to make the move as smooth, efficient, and fast as possible, Dale has enlisted his own team of movers.

When anyone in the church anticipates a move, they know to call Dale. That information almost seems to be part of what's shared in the new members' class. Some have jokingly said that young people have joined the church just so Dale could supervise their move. And some have been members, like Dale, for so long that he has now moved them several times.

Moving people is Dale's special ministry, but he's good at other things too. He doesn't like being in the limelight so you won't see him praying in church, but you will find him in Sunday School every Sunday, having studied his lesson and ready to contribute to the discussion. You'll always find him at the hospital when a member is sick and at the home and the funeral home when grieving members need his comforting presence. You won't find him in a leadership role or on the church council, but you will find him supporting his pastor, his church, and caring for members whenever a need occurs.

I think the early church would pick a guy like Dale for ministry. His church certainly appreciates all he does, especially his ministry of moving.

Read Acts 6:1-7. How is Dale ministering to people in his church? What needs is he meeting? How is administration part of his ministry?

If you want to know more about how deacons operate in your church, set an appointment with one to learn what he does. Listen for ways you can join with deacons in ministering to church and community members.

What issue in your church is causing or has potential to cause divisiveness? How can deacons help? Pray about this matter; then if God leads, talk about the matter with a deacon you know and trust.

A COMMUNITY OF PRIESTS

"But you are a chosen race, a royal priesthood, a holy nation, a people for His possession, so that you may proclaim the praises of the One who called you out of darkness into His marvelous light." *1 Peter 2:9*

God's heartbeat has never changed. From all eternity God has desired that every people and every person have the privilege of knowing Him as rightful King. Now as members of His kingdom, we have the privilege and responsibility of declaring His excellency among the nations.

We are special in His sight, not just so that we can bask in His blessing, but so we can be participants in His grand calling and Great Commission. May we ever be faithful to and thankful for this twin privilege and duty.

Eternal Impact, page 162

Many churches have shifted from singing hymns to singing choruses, and even those that sing hymns seldom sing some of the old standards. Yet we can learn a lot from the words of hymns and sometimes from the lives of those who wrote the instructive words. One example is "Give of Your Best to the Master."

The words of this old hymn were written by a New Yorker, Howard Benjamin Grose (1851–1939) who practiced what he wrote. Grose attended the University of Chicago and the University of Rochester. In 1883 he was ordained a Baptist minister and served as pastor of First Baptist Church, Poughkeepsie, New York, and First Baptist Church, Pittsburgh, Pennsylvania. He also served as president of the University of South Dakota; taught history at the University of Chicago; was assistant editor of *The Watchman* in Boston, editorial secretary for the American Baptist Home Mission Society, and editor of the *Missions* journal for twenty-three years.

His lifetime of service indicates that he lived his life giving his best to honor the King.

> Give of your best to the Master;
> Give of the strength of your youth.
> Throw your soul's fresh, glowing ardor
> Into the battle for truth.
> Jesus has set the example,
> Dauntless was He, young and brave.
> Give Him your loyal devotion;
> Give Him the best that you have.
>
> Give of your best to the Master;
> Give Him first place in your heart.
> Give Him first place in your service;
> Consecrate every part.
> Give, and to you will be given;
> God His beloved Son gave.
> Gratefully seeking to serve Him,
> Give Him the best that you have.
>
> Give of your best to the Master;
> Naught else is worthy His love.
> He gave Himself for your ransom,
> Gave up His glory above.
> Laid down His life without murmur,
> You from sin's ruin to save.
> Give Him your heart's adoration;
> Give Him the best that you have.

Read Romans 12:1. How do you serve God with your body?

Read Romans 15:16. How do you serve God with your ministry?

Read Hebrews 13:15. How do you serve God with your praise?

Read Hebrews 13:16. How do you serve God through good deeds?

Read Philippians 4:18. How do you serve God by sharing what you have with those in need?

GIFTED FOR SERVICE TO THE KING

"According to the grace given to us, we have different gifts."
Romans 12:6

> There are no spectators in the body of Christ. You were saved and gifted by God to serve in the advancement of the kingdom. … All members of the body must work together if the church is to operate with full effectiveness. The fact that all are gifted means that no one has all the gifts. You are important to the work of your church!
>
> *Eternal Impact*, page 164

Bill was a new believer. The change in his life was dramatic. People who knew the "old Bill" sometimes didn't recognize him when they saw him at work or the grocery or on the golf course. Some said he looked ten years younger. One thing was certain, his life was now filled with joy. He'd been a Christian for about six months now, and no one could remember seeing him without a smile on his face since that glorious day when he met Jesus.

Bill had been reading his Bible, going to church for Bible study, worship, and every other opportunity. Like a sponge, he wanted to absorb everything he could about God, Jesus, the Bible, and how he could best serve in God's kingdom. He'd talked with the pastor about how and where he could serve. He'd taken a gifts inventory, but that didn't clarify everything for him entirely about where he should serve. He and the pastor finally agreed that Bill could try different areas of service. As he served, he would recognize what fit and what didn't, and that would help him discover his gifts.

Everyone thought Bill would be a great basketball coach. But that didn't work as well as Bill thought it would. It turns out that he knew a lot more about what players ought to be doing from his recliner than from the sidelines. He felt like he was just confusing the kids. In fact, he felt pretty confused himself.

What about serving as an usher or a parking lot greeter? Bill liked that. He enjoyed being helpful and greeting people with a smile. OK, he'd found one thing he did well, but surely there was something more. He longed to do more.

One Sunday several preschool workers were out with the flu. Bill was at church early and didn't show signs of even a sniffle. Would he please work with the bed babies that Sunday? Bill was assured that others would be working alongside him if he needed help.

Bill's grandchildren lived three states away. He longed to see them more, especially since his life had changed so dramatically. As he held and rocked and sang to the babies that day, he thought of his grandkids so far away. His big hands were gentle, and his voice was soothing. Those who worked with him that Sunday remarked at the calm he brought to the preschool area. And Bill loved it too. Who would have guessed that loving babies was one of his special gifts?

Bill kept loving babies, serving as an usher, and looking for other ways to serve. And every time he finds another way to use what God has given him in kingdom service, his smile just keeps getting bigger.

Read 1 Corinthians 12:8-10; 12:28-29; Romans 12:6-8; and Ephesians 4:11. Make a list of all the gifts listed in these passages. You do not need to list more than once the ones that are repeated.

Mark through the gifts you have tested and know you don't have.

Circle the gifts you know you have.

Select one gift from the list that remains that you would like to test to see if you have. Talk with a church leader about trying a role that uses that gift to see if that is a way God wants you to serve in His kingdom.

THE BODY WORKING TOGETHER FOR KINGDOM GROWTH

"And He personally gave some to be apostles, some prophets, some evangelists, some pastors and teachers, for the training of the saints in the work of ministry, to build up the body of Christ." *Ephesians 4:11-12*

Unity is necessary for diversely gifted members to work together. One body member working alone can accomplish little. We are interdependent and thus inextricably bound together as we are united to the King. *Eternal Impact*, page 174

Most of the time, when our body is healthy and we are feeling fine, we don't pay much attention to various body parts or functions. But when something happens, we quickly realize how the body is fit together.

Have you ever been on crutches? Your foot or leg may hurt, but so do your arms from the extra work they are doing in place of your foot and leg. When you have a cold, not only your head suffers, but your whole body is tired and run down. And a stomach virus! When your stomach isn't working properly, you feel weak and frail.

And when you care for the injured body part, soon the entire body is feeling better. You can get on with life without thinking about how well your body is working for you.

A church can learn a lot from how the human body functions. Let's look at some applications.

1. The entire body, the church, works best when everyone is working well together. When a church has a mission, a vision, and goals, everyone can be united, going in the same direction doing kingdom work. When that happens, growth is sure to follow.

2. One part of the body can't do what another part was intended to do. Some people who have no hands have learned to do a lot with their feet. But that's not ideal. In a church some people will take on extra jobs to make sure everything gets done, but that's not the way it should be. All members should be using their gifts so that everyone has a part and

no one is experiencing burnout from carrying too heavy a load. The body works best when every member is active.

3. When the human body is sick, we take care of it until it is in working order again, doing whatever we can to preserve life and health. That's how we should take care of one another in the church. When one member has a problem, others should come alongside to help that person return to a healthy role in the community of faith. When clashes come among church members, the entire body should work together to restore unity, doing so in a spirit of love.

4. When one part of the body is weak, the body works together to strengthen it. Did you know that when you are weak or your body is stressed, your vocal cords have a hard time speaking? That's because they are under stress with the rest of the body in trying to bring healing. Sometimes church members make mistakes. They need encouragement and perhaps correction and accountability. They need grace not condemnation. They need love not judgment. When the body restores one of its members, the body is healthy and whole again.

Read Ephesians 3:14-21. What did Paul do for members of the church at Ephesus?

Pray for your congregation, for its leaders, for unity, for people to work together for kingdom growth.

Are there ways in which your church is not as healthy as it should be? How can you make a positive difference?

FROM OPPOSITION TO VICTORY

Viewer Guide

1. Our business is to advance God's _____ by His power and for His glory.

2. Continually focus on _____ and on the kingdom of God and its purposes.

3. Principles to Deal with Opposition

   • Look for God's _____.

   • Allow prayer and the _____ of the Holy Spirit

   to work.

   • Live with total _____.

   • Be bold in the declaration of God's _____.

   •Remain focused on the kingdom and leave the _____ to the King.

   • Stay committed to the _____.

   • Obey _____ Word.

4. Christ loves the church so much that He calls it to _____.

5. You can have eternal _____.

6

Notes

FROM OPPOSITION TO VICTORY

During this study what have you learned about what the Bible says about the early church?

What have you learned about your own church?

What have you learned about your own role in your church?

What action will you take to make a greater eternal impact through your church in your community and the world?

Watch this week's DVD.

1. Read Acts 6:1-7. How is your church organized to meet people's needs?

Read Acts 13:3. How is your church organized to reach people for Christ?

2. Read Acts 20:17-24. What opposition did leaders in the early church experience? How did they stay focused on their mission rather than the opposition? What opposition do churches in the twenty-first century experience? How can they stay focused on their mission? What is the same about the opposition the church faced two thousand years ago and today? What is different?

3. Read Ephesians 1:15-23. What did Paul pray for the church at Ephesus? If your church could do anything at all, with no thoughts of financial or human limits, what would you like to do?

Read Ephesians 1:3-14. What has God done for people and for the church? What is stopping your church (and others) from attempting great things for God? What can your church do to reach its potential?

4. Read Revelation 1:17-18. What is the good news Christ wanted John to write?

John highlighted things the churches were doing well: working hard, strong foundation, response to persecution, resolute faith, and others. As John wrote about the problems in the seven churches, he mentioned tolerating evil, false teachers/teaching, abandoning their first love, idol worship, immorality, and others.

What is your church doing well? What cautions do you think John might write, as Christ led, to warn your church about practices it needs to change?

Throughout Revelation, John calls the churches to remain faithful to God's Word. How is your church doing that?

John also seeks to encourage the churches. Do your leaders need encouragement? Plan a way to encourage them.

5. Read Ephesians 1:20-23. What did Paul write in these verses about the church and its Head? What power does Jesus have? How does Christ choose to work on earth?

That's reason to celebrate!

Make a list of recent praises about your church, its work, and individuals in it.

Pray, thanking God for working through your church.

ORGANIZED FOR KINGDOM ADVANCEMENT

"God is not a God of disorder but of peace." 1 Corinthians 14:33

Church governance is actually more implied in the New Testament than declared, which could explain why several different forms of governance are actually practiced by evangelical churches today. But whatever our form of governance, we should seek to apply biblical principles that allow us to conduct God's kingdom agenda in a manner consistent with His character.

Eternal Impact, page 177

A quiz show asked contestants to define "idiot's walk." According to the quiz show, "idiot's walk" is what you do in a hotel room after you are packed and ready to leave and turn in your key. It is a last look through the closet, drawers, under the bed. Sometimes this last look reveals not only your own shoes under the bed but also items left behind by previous occupants—a hat that has fallen behind a chair, a phone recharger still plugged into the electrical outlet on the desk, toothpaste in the bathroom, maybe jewelry in the hotel room safe. Even organized travelers do well to take one more look.

With the complexity of travel today, it's easy to feel like an idiot. Airport rules seem to change every time you fly, even if you fly frequently. And if you travel internationally, you face more challenges than language barriers.

But there are tools to help travelers stay organized—checklists for packing, Internet instructions for current airline and airport rules and regulations, signs everywhere, and sometimes even volunteers at airports to help confused passengers. Travel magazines are filled with pitfalls to avoid and tips to make travel a success. And if you drive, you don't even need a map anymore if you use a GPS. It will direct, even redirect you, in a courteous voice from your driveway to your destination.

We live in a complex world. Travel is one area of complexity. Church is another. Once upon a time, a member of a church in one state could go to a church of the same denomination in another and feel right at home. The music, the style of worship, the Sunday School literature, and even the church polity would be pretty much the same. But this isn't true any longer. Even small churches seem to be complex organizations.

Thom Rainer, president of LifeWay Christian Resources, wrote a book, *Simple Church*. The point of the book is that churches don't need to keep adding more and more layers to reach people for Christ and make disciples. Churches can simplify in order to focus on the main reason for their existence—fulfilling Jesus' command to go into all the world to teach the Gospel and baptize believers.

How is your church organized? Is it complex? Is it fulfilling the Great Commission, reaching people for Christ and growing disciples? Maybe it's time to simplify.

Just as your priorities are evident by looking at your checkbook and your calendar, your church's priorities are evident by looking at the church budget and the schedule of programs and events. Take a fresh look at your church budget and calendar. What priorities do you see?

Take an idiot's walk around your church, looking at it with fresh eyes. Does it give the appearance of being organized for ministry? If not, how can you help improve the situation?

Keep in mind your small group discussion of the following verses. Now read them again and think about your specific role.

Read Acts 6:1-7. How is your church organized to meet people's needs? What is your role in meeting people's needs?

Read Acts 13:3. How is your church organized to reach people for Christ? How do you reach people for Christ?

How do you participate in your church's plan of cooperation to do more than you or your church alone can do?

At what points do you fit in your church's organization? Should you be involved in additional areas of your church?

PERSEVERE IN THE FACE OF OPPOSITION

"The Holy Spirit testifies to me that chains and afflictions are waiting for me. But I count my life of no value to myself, so that I may finish my course and the ministry I received from the Lord Jesus, to testify to the gospel of God's grace." Acts 20:23-24

> In your journey to be a kingdom-centered church and forge crowns for the King, you will face obstacles that could cause you to lose focus and to lose heart. Persevere! Let nothing deter you! The cause of the kingdom is worth the cost!   *Eternal Impact*, page 189

In the suburbs of a city in the Bible Belt, two churches that were once evangelical churches are no more. Were they church plants that failed? No. Were they churches that didn't transition well in a changing neighborhood and gradually lost all their members? No. Were they churches that refused to change to meet the needs of people today? No. They were churches that let opposition destroy them from within.

One of the churches apparently disagreed about which gifts were better and whether some members would be allowed to have a private prayer language. Over time the disputes surrounding these issues caused more and more people to leave the church until one day passersby were surprised to see a For Sale sign at the church.

The other church was thriving and decided to build a new building. But disagreements arose during the building process. Some members became angry about decisions that were made, and they quit giving. The church quickly became overextended and could not meet its financial obligations. A For Sale sign appeared on this property, too.

People in the communities were surprised. What had happened? Other churches were thriving because these churches were both located in growing parts of town. New church plants had popped up everywhere. Surely these new churches would soon fill the buildings left behind when their congregations disbanded.

But this was not to be. One of those evangelical churches is now a Hindu temple. The other is a Unity church. Buildings that once were filled with God's praises and prayers in Jesus' name have become filled with people who worship but do not know the one true God.

Hard to believe, but this is what opposition can do in a church. Greed, power, control—the devil can destroy a church with these.

Opposition can come from within the church or from the outside. Either way, the church's response to opposition should be to draw together in unity and love. What might have happened in these two churches if love of God, love of one another, and a desire to stay focused on mission had prevailed? No closed doors. No For Sale signs. No lack of a witness in these communities. But a continued clear call to come to Jesus would have prevailed.

Read Acts 16:25. Paul and Silas faced opposition, imprisonment, and other hardships as they preached and shared good news of Jesus Christ, just as their church had commissioned them to do. What opposition is your church facing from within and without? Pray without ceasing that your church will overcome this opposition.

Read Acts 20:26-27. Is your church consistently teaching God's Word? Are leaders living lives of integrity? Pray for your leaders that they will be strong and accountable.

UNLEASHED TO EXPRESS THE FULLNESS OF GOD

"And He put everything under His feet and appointed Him as head over everything for the church, which is His body, the fullness of the One who fills all things in every way." *Ephesians 1:22-23*

Wisdom is the God-given ability to use the spiritual knowledge gained as the Holy Spirit gives understanding of the promises of God. We sometimes fail to realize our potential because we fail to understand all that has been made available to us in Christ.

Eternal Impact, page 192

When Jane Creswell was a college student, she spent a summer in Alabama working with the children of seasonal workers in farm country. She observed that if the farmers were kind to the workers, the children were more receptive to her as she taught Bible stories, sang songs, played games, and did crafts projects. She was good at her work, and her supervisor told her that she should consider becoming a vocational missionary. But Jane said no; God was calling her to be a missionary in the corporate world. Observations she had about the connection between kindness and the next generation's response to the Gospel would serve her well as a manager at IBM and later as that company's first internal coach.

Jane is now a full-time team coach. She works with large corporations as well as ministry teams. Through coaching, even more than through her corporate job, she finds ways to model Christian living as well as to share the Gospel.

Coaching and Christian leadership fit well together. Both focus on individual responsibility and maximizing potential. As a Christian coach working with ministry teams, Jane has opportunities to help people reach for God-sized tasks, accomplishing goals they never would have believed possible. And they do them using the gifts God has given them and all the resources God makes available to them as they claim His promises and attempt great things for the kingdom.

Jane has recently had opportunities to work with international missionaries through Southern Baptists' International Mission Board. And she has attempted some God-sized tasks of her own, adding writing books to her impressive resume, something she couldn't imagine doing without God's help. Her first book was *Christ-Centered Coaching*. Her *Complete Idiot's Guide to Coaching for Excellence* is scheduled for release on October 15, 2008.

By the way, Jane married the kind farmer's son.

Read Ephesians 1:15-19. Paul prayed for the members of the church. List his requests of God on their behalf.

Read Ephesians 1:3-14. What has God done for you? What resources are available to you?

If you could attempt your greatest dream of service in God's kingdom, what would it be?

What is the first step you can take to make this dream a reality?

Pray for God to show you the way.

A WORD OF WARNING

"But I have this against you: you have abandoned the love you had at first. Remember then how far you have fallen; repent." *Revelation 2:4-5*

In the book of Revelation, John provides a glimpse of his vision of the risen Lord. . . . The first part of this vision, we know, was made up of "letters" to . . . the seven angels of the seven churches. The term angel translates the word meaning "messenger." It appears likely here that angel stands for the earthly messenger who was the recipient of the letter, probably the pastoral leader of the church. The churches themselves are pictured as lampstands, with Christ Himself being the light. I love that image. The church is to be the earthly platform through which God reveals the glory of His Son.

Perhaps most beautiful of all, however, is that Christ is depicted as walking among the lampstands, indicating His love and care for His church. Both His commendation and His warnings issue from His great love for His bride.

Eternal Impact, page 197

A friend tells this story about a mission trip to Korea.

We knew, of course, that Korea has many Christians. We were excited about the opportunity to work with the churches to try to reach people for Christ and to learn from the dynamic believers in this country. We also had some concerns, as most people generally do on short-term missions trips, about wanting to do our work well, overcoming language barriers, staying well, eating unusual food.

After our long flights, we descended after dark to the city of Seoul. We boarded a bus and watched, wide eyed, as we approached our hotel for that night. We saw lively nighttime street markets and other scenes of the city. But what caught our eye and warmed our hearts were the neon crosses we began to see everywhere. In the crowded city not many churches meet in a recognizable church building, but wherever they meet, the red cross sits atop that building. We saw one, then another, then many. What a reassuring sight! We felt an immediate connection with our Korean brothers and sisters in Christ.

After a day of preparation in Seoul, we left for our assigned church in a farming community. Our church had a fairly traditional church building with the now familiar red neon cross on top.

As we visited homes to share our testimonies, we observed the Koreans who worked with us persuasively explaining the good news. Some accepted Christ, and some did not. I'm confident those church members will return again to any who did not accept Christ. On one home visit, we talked with a woman who lived in a modern home but washed her clothes in a nearby stream. We shared our testimony and the plan of salvation, and our translator, a student, did his best to repeat what we had said. Even though we could not understand her words, by the way her face lit up, we clearly understood that she was accepting Christ as her personal Savior.

We came home from that trip carrying the light of Christ even brighter because of the example of the Korean Christians. They work hard and long to reach people for Christ. They pray and pray and pray and they worship joyfully. We were inspired to lay aside our excuses and the busyness that gets in our way and to focus, as Paul did, on working through our church and telling others the good news about Jesus.

Read Revelation 2:2-3. Christ commended the church at Ephesus. What qualities did He commend? What qualities would Christ commend in you?

Read Revelation 2:4-5. Christ also rebuked the church at Ephesus. What qualities might He rebuke in you?

Read Revelation 22:5. What promise do you find here? How will you let Christ's light shine in you now?

A KINGDOM CELEBRATION

"Therefore, since we are receiving a kingdom that cannot be shaken, let us hold on to grace. By it, we may serve God acceptably, with reverence and awe." Hebrews 12:28

Are you beginning to understand why Christ loves the church? Are you beginning to see what is at stake? Yes, I am talking about your church—the church you attend each Sunday. Your church is crucial to the work of the King until He returns. It can and must play a pivotal role in the reaching of your Jerusalem, Judea, Samaria, and the ends of the earth. You must think strategically in all these areas, giving of yourself and your material resources joyously and sacrificially to advance His kingdom until He comes. God has created the world with resources sufficient for the advance of the Gospel to the ends of the earth. He has given a portion of those resources to you in stewardship, allowing you the privilege of participating in the greatest event in time and eternity—the coming of His kingdom. *Eternal Impact*, page 206

The 1984 movie, *Places in the Heart*, is the story of a woman in Texas in 1935. After her husband dies, Edna Spalding, played by Sally Field, faces one problem after another in her attempt to keep her farm and her children—a tornado, racial tension, and depression-era financial woes when the bottom falls out of the cotton market. She receives help from some unexpected sources, and those who might have helped did nothing at all. Some even snickered at her behind her back as she attempted to provide for her family in a man's world. In spite of everything, Edna prevails.

The final scene shows Edna and her boys at church one Sunday, a Sunday when the church is celebrating the Lord's Supper. As the camera pans the crowd, you begin to see all the characters in the film—friends and enemies, living and dead, black and white—take communion together at a church service. The scene seemed to say not only has Edna prevailed, but the little church has also prevailed in spite of the depression, in spite of interpersonal conflict, in spite of members' sins, in spite of death and hardship.

Christ's church prevails, and we, His children, should celebrate! When we come together as a church, to celebrate the Lord's Supper, to celebrate progress in reaching people around the world for Christ, or simply to enjoy a time of fellowship, it is time for us to put aside differences and disagreements, hurt feelings and perceived slights, and unite in Christian love.

The church is made up of God's people, all flawed; but we have a flawless Savior who loves us, who loves His church, and who provides all that we need to complete His mission to go into all the world and preach the Gospel.

Read Matthew 24:14. What "in spite of's" did the early church face? Yet the church prevailed. What are some "in spite of's" that the church faces today? Yet the church prevails. That's reason to celebrate!

Make a list of the good things about the church that you have learned from God's Word. Thank God for every one of them.

Make a list of all the good things about your church. Thank God for every one of them.

Make a list of your personal blessings from your church and individuals in it. Thank God for every one of them.

COMMITMENT AND CELEBRATION

Read Acts 2:44-47.

Think about your dreams for your church as you watch this week's DVD segment.

Brainstorm characteristics of the early church highlighted in this study.

Which characteristic is most meaningful to you personally? Why?

Which characteristic of your church is most like the New Testament church?

Which characteristic of the early church would you most like your church to develop?

How do you think your church can do this?

List your ideas for how your church can fulfill the new work you believe God is calling your church to do.

What difference would this change in your church make in your life? in your community? in God's kingdom?

How can you personally help your church go in this new direction?

Write a prayer here, thanking God for your church. Include in your prayer your desire to do what He wants you to do in His church.

Notes:

Other resources for eternal impact by Ken Hemphill

EMPOWERING KINGDOM GROWTH

This life-changing book about the meaning and power of God's kingdom is the basis for a *40-Day Experience*. Ken Hemphill, whose impact has been felt as an author, a pastor, and a seminary president, explains how God's deep passion for us gives us the key to a life with eternal purpose and meaning.

EKG, The Heartbeat of God, Hardcover Book
Item 978-0-8054-3147-6

EKG, The Heartbeat of God, Member Book
Item 978-0-6331-9758-2

EKG, The Heartbeat of God, DVD
Item 978-0-6331-9759-9

EKG, The Heartbeat of God, Leader Kit
Item 978-0-6331-9757-5

www.empoweringkingdomgrowth.com